TROWBRIDGE
THEN & NOW
IN COLOUR

MICHAEL MARSHMAN & KEN ROGERS

The
History
Press

First published in 2012

The History Press
The Mill, Brimscombe Port
Stroud, Gloucestershire, GL5 2QG
www.thehistorypress.co.uk

British Library Cataloguing in Publication Data.
A catalogue record for this book is available from the British Library.

ISBN 978 0 7524 7477 9

Typesetting and origination by The History Press
Manufacturing managed by Jellyfish Print Solutions Ltd
Printed in India.

CONTENTS

ABOUT THE AUTHORS

Fascinated by the history of Trowbridge, Michael Marshman was born and grew up there. He went on to work locally as a librarian and later became County Local Studies Librarian. He currently works at the Wiltshire & Swindon History Centre at Chippenham, and specialises in village history and interpretation.

Ken Rogers was born in Trowbridge and later returned to the town to become County Archivist. He is now retired but continues to be interested in local history, specialising in the Wiltshire and Somerset cloth industry. This is the fourth book he has co-authored with Michael on the history of Trowbridge.

INTRODUCTION

Trowbridge, like many small towns, has changed greatly in some areas since the 1950s, when the most recent of the old photographs in this book were taken. At that time it was an industrial and market town with four working cloth factories, a substantial food processing industry, several light engineering businesses and many small shops. The weekly livestock market – a treat for town children who did not normally see many farm animals – was accompanied by many stalls in the large market hall.

The tightly-knit town had People's Park and Flower Show Field but few other open spaces apart from the recently demolished 'slums' of the Conigre. The town's administration was carried out by an urban district council with offices in the Town Hall. County government had been centred in the town since 1889, which created lots of employment opportunities, and many young people went straight from the two high schools into County Hall. There were plenty of jobs at this time and few young people left their native town.

The population of Trowbridge had grown to around 15,000 by the late 1950s, most of them living in the nineteenth-century terraces built for factory workers or on the twentieth-century council estates. Ribbon development with larger houses had occurred along the main roads but the large private housing estates were still to come. People knew, personally, by sight or by reputation, many of their fellow townspeople. The George was the main inn and social centre. There were two large 1930s cinemas; a football club, which attracted over 2,000 people at times; allotments, which men dug at weekends; and much good community spirit, perhaps inherited from togetherness during the dark days of war.

Parts of modern Trowbridge show the effect of the post-war popularity of the internal combustion engine. Roads have been widened, and houses and gardens flattened to provide car parks. Also, having the means to get to work where you do not live causes much congestion. Some landmark buildings are gone – an ancient rectory, the Roundstone Hotel, the buildings behind the façades of the George and Market House, an armoury and a couple of early nineteenth-century factories. Whole terraces have gone, while some roads have been driven through others. Trinity Church and the early nineteenth-century Longfield House are now isolated in the middle of two roundabouts. Fortunately, we still have many old buildings and some fine ones from the eighteenth century.

New housing estates encompass the town and, encouragingly, good modern housing has been built in areas where earlier housing had long gone, such as the Conigre, Duke Street and Prospect Place. Very few industries from the mid twentieth century remain, and most public and commercial buildings have new uses. In common with most towns, few independent shops survive – H.J. Knee's, the United Kingdom's longest established family-owned department store, being a large and notable exception – and many of the pubs have closed, although the number of cafés and restaurants has increased.

Opposite: Trowbridge celebrates the coronation of King George VI in style,
Wednesday, 12 May 1937.

THE MARKET PLACE

TROWBRIDGE'S MARKET
PLACE was laid out as part of the
development of a new borough
outside the defences of the castle in
around 1250, the year the grant of a
right to hold a market was obtained.
A church on the site of St James's
was probably provided at this time to
replace one inside the castle, but the
earliest part of the present building
is the tower and spire, built in the
fourteenth century. When the old
photograph was taken, H.J. Knee
still occupied the ancient building
in which they had started in 1879.
The George was still the town's main
hotel, and J. Avons and Son made their
brushes in a factory in Court Street.

H.J. KNEE LEFT their old premises in 1936 and Burton, the outfitter's, replaced it with the present structure. Next door, another outfitters' shop, Foster's, replaced the handsome Victorian façade with a pathetic 'modern' frontage. The ancient building occupied by Avons and Son went in 1926, and the 'Tudor' group that replaced it was hailed in the local press 'as in days of old'. We tend to mock such pretensions today, but at least it has more character than Foster's gave us.

MARKET HOUSE AND THE TOWN HALL

APART FROM A market cross, removed in around
1780, Trowbridge had no market buildings until
1861, when, as you can read around its capital arch,
William Stancomb, the lord of the manor, erected the
building nearest to the camera. It was not a gift to the
town: for some years Stancomb took the income from
the letting of stalls in it and finally sold it to the Local
Board of Health in 1892.

The Town Hall was given to the town by Roger –
later Sir Roger – Brown to mark the Golden Jubilee
of Queen Victoria and opened in 1889. Until 1974 it
provided offices for the local authority (Trowbridge
Urban District Council), court rooms and a large
hall for all kinds of social functions, including such
diverse events as photographic exhibitions and Top
Twenty dances.

TODAY'S PICTURE SHOWS the entrance to Castle Place, a shopping precinct that was built on the site of the former market yard in 1973. The large hall in which the indoor market had been held went too, but the façade was converted to a Weatherspoon's pub named after the town's most famous native, Sir Isaac Pitman of shorthand fame.

The Town Hall passed to the West Wiltshire District Council in 1974 and was then sold to the county council for use as magistrates' courts. After some years it was found that it did not conform to modern standards, and at the moment the future of the hall is in doubt. In spite of what Pevsner called its 'wild Franco-Elizabethan' style, it is a much valued feature of Trowbridge today.

UPPER FORE STREET
AND THE TOWN HALL

THIS VIEW WAS taken before 1906, when the furthest house on the right was removed to make Market Street wider. Nearest the camera on that side are adjoining boot and shoe shops, Tucker's and the Public Benefit Boot Co., both adorned with rows of what were, no doubt, gas lamps.

Further along, Saxty was a draper and outfitter. Opposite, Massey and Browne was a ladies' outfitter. The tall narrow frontage of the Market Tavern dated from 1801, at which time it was called the Cross Keys.

THIS PART OF Fore Street is now limited to pedestrians during the day. Apart from the Town Hall, only three buildings remain: what used to be the Public Benefit Boot Co. on the right, the adjoining shop to its left, and what was once Massey and Browne. The Market Tavern was closed as a pub in 1971, demolished when White Hart Yard was made in 1979 and rebuilt more or less in facsimile. The door and shop window of the old building can be seen in the Trowbridge Museum. In front of this building stands the town's only Victorian pillar box. It is a sign of the times that in this photograph three of the buildings are charity shops and one is empty.

THE MARKET PLACE AND THE GEORGE

A TAVERN ON the site of the George belonged to a man who died of the Black Death in 1349, and the name 'The George' is recorded in 1469. It faced the busy market place and was opposite the remains of the castle. The inn was the centre of Trowbridge's social life for centuries, being the venue in the eighteenth century for many events, including coronation feasts, concerts and assemblies. It ceased to be a hotel in 1969 and was finally closed as a public house in 1980. To its right, a large Georgian house stands on the site of a

burgage tenement given to Lacock Abbey before 1243. The house was built in around 1730 for John Watts, a retired Portugal merchant.

THE BUILDINGS APPEAR little changed since the 1950s view. In fact, the George was demolished in 1982, when parts of an earlier building were found behind the stone façade (some painted plaster is on display in the museum). However, owing to the Trowbridge Civic Society, the façade was saved and rebuilt. In its present form it dates from around 1860. The pedestrianisation of this part of Fore Street has enabled the coffee shops to have tables outside and outdoor functions to be held here.

THE WOOLPACK

THE HISTORY OF the Woolpack – another principle inn during the eighteenth and nineteenth centuries – is not as clear as that of the George on the opposite side of the market place. It was probably licensed as early as the seventeenth century and was also a social centre, a typical event being a theatrical performance in 1804 for which a poster still exists. The Woolpack was also the starting point for the first direct coach service from Trowbridge to London in 1753,

and it remained the main coaching inn until the 1790s; later, coach services generally ran from the George.

THE WOOLPACK WAS demolished in 1913 to make way for the town's first purpose-built cinema, the Picture Palace. This was rebuilt as the Gaumont in 1937 and later renamed the Odeon. The cinema closed in 1971 and was demolished to make way for the present building with the bland façade, which was used briefly by a Richway supermarket, and then, since 1976, as the main entrance for Trowbridge's wonderful department store, Knee's, founded in 1879.

CORNER OF CASTLE STREET
AND MARKET STREET

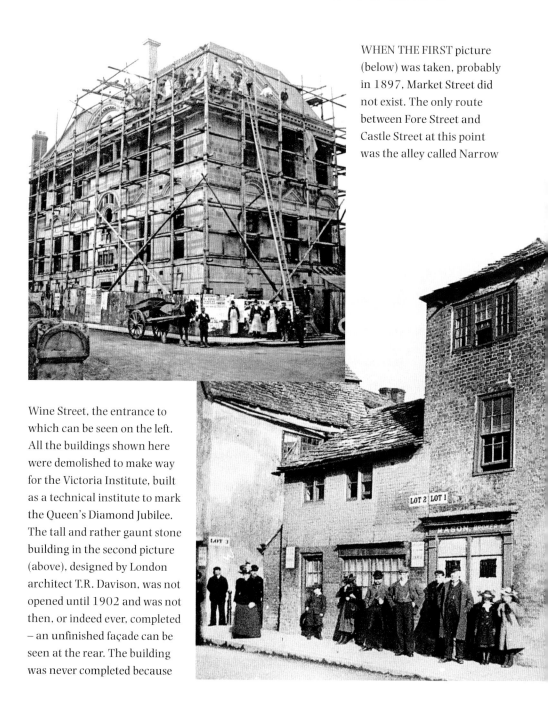

WHEN THE FIRST picture (below) was taken, probably in 1897, Market Street did not exist. The only route between Fore Street and Castle Street at this point was the alley called Narrow Wine Street, the entrance to which can be seen on the left. All the buildings shown here were demolished to make way for the Victoria Institute, built as a technical institute to mark the Queen's Diamond Jubilee. The tall and rather gaunt stone building in the second picture (above), designed by London architect T.R. Davison, was not opened until 1902 and was not then, or indeed ever, completed – an unfinished façade can be seen at the rear. The building was never completed because

the money ran out: the architect had wanted to build cheaply using brick with terracotta dressings but this was rejected as being out of keeping with Trowbridge's older buildings.

THE VICTORIA INSTITUTE was used for varying educational purposes, including the two county secondary schools, the County Textile School and the Victoria Commercial School, until 1969. Today it might well have been converted for accommodation, although this would have been awkward as there was no ground floor, only stairs inside the front door leading down to a semi-basement and up to the first floor. It was demolished in 1984 and was largely unmissed, even by conservationists. This commanding site, looking down Castle Street, deserved something better than the small, bland shops that were built here.

MARKET STREET

THE OLD PHOTOGRAPH from the 1950s gives us another view of the Victoria Institute's unfinished rear to the right, and the adjoining tin shed, which, in 1961, the Trowbridge Council tried to get removed as they felt it was an eyesore. To the left is the five-arched façade of Market House, erected in 1861. Straight ahead the Court Hall is seen, the view partially obscured by the ladies' lavatories. The Court Hall was built in 1854 as a meeting place for the County Court and the Mechanics' Institute. In the late 1860s, however, it was replaced as

a social centre by Hill's Hall in Silver Street, and in 1874 the building became a warehouse for a firm of cloth merchants instead.

THE ARCHED FRONT part of the Market House remains but the market hall, which contained the stalls of market traders and entertaining cheapjacks on market days, went when the Castle Place shopping precinct was made in 1973. The front part has become the Sir Isaac Pitman public house and restaurant, run by national chain Weatherspoon's. The lavatories went in 1973 as well, which gave the street its present width, allowing its use as a bus terminus to resume. The Court Hall, used between 1946 and 1994 as a restaurant, is a shoe shop at present.

CORNER OF MARKET STREET AND FORE STREET

THE OLD PHOTOGRAPH was taken to show the brand new building put up in 1936 for the International Stores, a national chain of grocery shops. It replaced a plain Georgian building but, owing to some quirk of property ownership, a little part of the old structure survived at the right-hand side and remained for many years one of the town's architectural oddities. To the right we see a pair of houses that date from the 1790s and are very similar in style to those still standing in The Halve. When this picture was taken, the ground floor was divided between a motor showroom and a hairdresser's.

THE INTERNATIONAL STORES closed in 1975, and since then the building has been used by
the Abbey National Building Society, later Abbey National (now Santander) bank. The Georgian
buildings on the right were demolished in 1960 and replaced by the building shown, used firstly
as a Fine Fare supermarket, then by Boots the chemist. When Boots moved to the Shires Gateway
in 2011, Lloyd's chemists expanded, moving into Boots' vacant premises.

CORNER OF CASTLE STREET AND FORE STREET

THE SITE ON which the two buildings seen here being demolished once stood came onto the market in 1886 and was bought by William Walker, a prominent member of the Local Board of Health, so that the entrance to Castle Street could be widened. We can also see the front of a two-gabled shop, at that time occupied by James Beaven, an ironmonger.

THE MODERN PHOTOGRAPH shows the four-storied shop built on the corner in 1887 and, largely hidden by the tree, the adjoining building that Beaven's successors, Burgess and Co., put up around 1890. Both are good examples of the vogue at that time for having display windows on upper floors. Knee's used the corner building from 1887 and acquired the adjoining one in 1894; this remained the main site of their department store until 1977, when they concentrated on their present premises on the other side of Red Hat Lane, behind the earlier store.

MANVERS STREET LOOKING FROM FORE STREET

THE OLD PHOTOGRAPH on the right dates from around 1900, when the public house on the right was still called the Three Tuns Inn. It was later renamed the Red Lion and eventually closed in 1958. Conversion into a shop then revealed that the plain eighteenth-century frontage hid a timber-framed structure from the Tudor period. Vincent's butchers still had its bow-windowed shopfront at this time.

THE MODERN PHOTOGRAPH shows that Vincent's shopfront has been replaced and the building next to the former public house modernised. The partial pedestrianisation of the upper part of Fore Street has allowed a tree to be planted, which largely hides the fact that the buildings in this part of the street are little changed, other than in the usage. This street does show the pleasing combination of stone and birch buildings that are a feature of Trowbridge town centre. The factory chimney, like all others in the town, is long gone.

FORE STREET AND MANVERS STREET CORNER

THESE BUILDINGS ARE shown with celebratory decorations, probably either for the laying of the foundation stone of the Town Hall in 1887, or for its opening in 1889. The lower building to the left is much older than its exterior suggests. The stone façade of around 1700 hides the timber-framed house of the Langford family, among the town's wealthiest clothiers in Tudor times. Nearer the camera, the L-shaped building is made of brick, which, in the eighteenth century, was

unusual for a building of this sophistication. It is believed to date from 1736. To the right we can see the Auction Mart of 1872.

ONE HUNDRED AND twenty years on from the earlier picture, the buildings differ only in detail. The older one has had its stone tiles replaced by pantiles and has been used as a café called The Crowing Cock since 1947. The other has lost its attic floor entirely, in favour of a flat roof. The bow-window was put on in the 1960s for an off-licence. The Auction Mart has gone, but still standing nearby is a former printing works, later the motor showroom of A.A. Bodman.

27

FORE STREET LOOKING FROM MANVERS STREET

ON THE LEFT the two-gabled building has imitation timber framing, put on quite recently when this picture was taken in the 1920s. It is in fact a genuinely old building, sixteenth

century or earlier. The eighteenth-
and nineteenth-century façades
on the right of the picture are
also quite likely to hide some
timber-framed buildings. The
military wagon reminds us that
Trowbridge was a garrison town;
the men would have been members
of the Royal Horse Artillery,
stationed at Trowbridge Barracks.

THE AGREEABLE MIXTURE of
buildings from various periods
remains little changed; only the
building on the very right of the
old picture has been replaced.
Whether the flower baskets and trees
improve the town centre is a matter
of opinion. The street furniture
certainly does not.

No. 68 FORE STREET

THIS HOUSE, DATING from around 1720, is one of a group of Georgian houses on the north side of the lower part of Fore Street known as the Parade. It was occupied by a succession of clothiers, ending with Samuel Salter, who died in 1850 leaving a personal estate of £350,000, and much property besides. After a period as a solicitors' office, and temporary use as the office of the Trowbridge Water Co. in 1874, it was converted for retail use by William Baxter, a china and

glass merchant, and Staffordshire warehouseman. He had been in business previously on at least three other sites in the town, having risen by his own industry and perseverance in his native London from being a machine boy in a printing firm. He died in 1883, aged sixty. Baxter's Arcade ran round three sides of the building and extended as far as Manvers Street. It is not known how much alteration was required to the façades.

IN THE TWENTIETH century, No. 68 was part of an almost continuous row of offices of Usher's Brewery that ran from Manvers Street to Wicker Hill, forming a labyrinth of stairs, passages and odd corners. Ushers were careful owners, especially after the publication of Pevsner's *Buildings of Wiltshire*, which described the Parade as 'a stretch of palaces' and led to their stonework being cleaned. The 1880 picture gives a glimpse of an old house behind, which was demolished in 1913 to enable the brewery, which had grown upon the former gardens of the houses, to be extended. The visible corner of it was given a Baroque cladding so as not to spoil the appearance of the adjoining houses. To the right, both views show the side of No. 67 Fore Street, with a stone façade of around 1700 hiding the Tudor clothier's house of the Langford family. The brewery closed in 2000, and No. 68 is now the offices of a charity.

THE PARADE LOOKING
DOWN TO WICKER HILL

THE EARLIEST MAPS of the town, from around 1780, show the houses on the right set back from the street just as they are now. The trees in our early twentieth-century view were removed in the interests of car parking in the 1920s. Behind them we can see that two of the houses then had dwarf walls and iron railings in front; these must have been removed for scrap in the Second World War. Parade House, to the right, has no visible railings, but we know from other pictures that it had them on the upper half of its frontage, and that the gate pillars were then to the right.

THE PRESENT DAY picture shows the sequence of three large Georgian houses: Arlington House to the left and Parade House to the right, both built in the early eighteenth century; between them is No. 72 Fore Street, built in 1794 to house Trowbridge's first bank. Parade House now has a complete set of iron railings and central gate pillars. A very pleasing feature of the Parade is the survival of a cobbled (locally known in the past as 'pitched') path running in front of the houses.

THE PARADE LOOKING UP FROM WICKER HILL

THIS PICTURE SHOWS buildings seen in previous pictures from a different angle: the Georgian façades of Nos 67 and 68 Fore Street, and the splendid frontage of the clothier's house that became a bank. Although this area of Fore Street is known as the Parade, possibly from townsfolk parading there on Sundays or maybe from military parades, it is still reckoned

The Parade Trowbridge

to be part of Fore Street, as it was in the 1870s. Unlike many Trowbridge streets, Fore Street still has its original numeration, going along one side and then back along the other, so No. 1 is on the right and No. 75 on the left of this picture, taken in around 1905.

EVERY BUILDING IN the earlier picture still stands. The most recent in date is the nearest to us on the right, built, or at least re-fronted, in the 1870s. The tallest building, further up on the same side, is the former office block of Samuel Salter and Co., cloth manufacturer of Home Mills, put up in 1864. The frontage closest to us on the left dates from 1844 but conceals what is left of a much earlier building, once a pub called Nonsuch or The Bell; it was partly demolished in 1844 to allow road widening. On the right, a former shopfront was removed in 1957, and the frontage is now on a building in Frome.

SILVER STREET FROM THE TOWN HALL

SEVERAL BUILDINGS ON the left of this pre-First World War picture were built in the 1840s and '60s as shops with accommodation or storage above. Dotesio and Todd were well-known printers in the town and had their stationary and book retail outlet here. The shop housed an office for the public to make telephone calls (standard public telephone kiosks were only first introduced in 1920). The projecting building beyond was replaced in 1932 by one of a similar design but on the same street line as its neighbours. On the right-hand side were gent's outfitters Wilkins and Co. and an ironmonger's shop; in 1920 Fear Hills moved across the street into this building and Hill's Hall behind, which had

been the main public hall in Victorian times. They went on to create a department store, concentrating mainly on clothes, furniture, china and household goods.

TODAY SILVER STREET is still a major shopping street but there have been many changes. Wilkins, becoming Wilkins and Darking, moved further down the street into Pitman House with the Trowbridge Music Saloon; the façade of this building was re-modelled in 1939. Both businesses have gone but next door the shop of H.B. Pitt is still going strong; a previous owner, Fred Pitt, was an avid collector of all materials relating to Trowbridge's history. Fear Hills remained a major store in the town for much of the twentieth century; on the other side of the street, the demolition of the New Inn and the eighteenth-century Presbyterian chapel (the town's public library in the 1950s) provided the site for a large Co-operative department store. Nearer the camera we can see that the replacement building of 1932 is more attractive than its predecessor. In the foreground on the right, Aplin's chemist shop was taken over by Lloyd's Chemist but still retains the tape on its top-floor windows, which was placed there in the Second World War to prevent glass fragments blowing inwards in the case of a bomb blast.

PARRISS'S CORNER,
SILVER STREET

WHEN THE OLD photograph on the left was taken in the 1930s, this site was known as Parriss's Corner, after the then owner of the long-standing ironmonger's business. We can see, however, that Mr Parriss kept up with the times when we read the signs 'Radio Corner' and 'The House for Wireless'. High quality toys also featured: boys could buy Frank Hornby's Meccano and his 0 gauge electric trains. From 1938, these became half the size at 00 guage, and in the 1950s were bought at Stroud Sims' shop in Stallard Street.

THE GRACEFUL OLD building gave way to its chunky successor in 1973. Particularly regretted was the loss of the Regency shopfront, a feature of which was the curved pane of plate glass seen behind the lamp post in the old photograph. Silver Street itself was one of the streets of medieval Trowbridge, connecting the important early routes of Fore Street and Church Street, then known as Back Street.

ROUNDSTONE STREET

THIS STREET TAKES its name from a landmark that stood in the road, or near its junction with Polebarn Road. Except for the building visible at the right margin, with the man leaning against it, every building in this pre-1914 photograph remains today. The plain stone terrace nearest the camera on the left dates from 1884, and the more elaborate one of brick with stone dressings, called Victoria Buildings, from the jubilee year of 1897. They replaced a row of much earlier houses, dating from the early eighteenth century, of which no photograph has so far been found. On the right is a group of three stone houses built in the 1790s; beyond the houses, the trees behind the iron railings were in the garden of Rodney House, built in 1790.

THE BUILDING AGAINST which we see the man leaning in our old view was one of the town's best Victorian ones, built in 1864 as a wine merchant's premises and later used as the Roundstone Hotel. It gave way in 1964 to our worst 'modern' building, the execrable post office. This setting back from the road revealed the wide end wall of the 1790s group of houses.

ROUNDSTONE STREET FROM POLEBARN HOUSE

TAKEN IN THE early 1950s, this view of Roundstone Street, looking the other way from the last photograph on page 40, shows buildings little changed from today's view. The area to the left, used at the time as it is now for short-term car parking, was provided in 1936 by removing the front garden of Rodney House, which became the offices of the Trowbridge Co-operative Society. The small shops on the other side of the road provided enjoyable browsing for a range of goods – now usually bought by a single visit to a supermarket.

THE 1950S PICTURE shows how the removal of the garden revealed the side wall of one of the

Georgian houses on the south side of the street, previously concealed by trees. As the modern
image here shows, in recent years the Trowbridge Civic Society have carried out imaginative
and effective improvements to the street: the wall is now decorated with a trompe l'oeil painting
of a Georgian façade, with panelled door, sash windows, real railings and a basket for a lantern,
which was saved from another house in the town. (The painted doorway can be seen just above
the top of the parked cars.) The Chinese restaurant is on the site of the first one to open in
Trowbridge in the 1960s.

POLEBARN HOUSE AND THE CARPENTERS' ARMS

THE CAPTION ON this old postcard reads 'Hilperton Road', but in fact Marlborough Buildings on the right have been numbered in Roundstone Street since they were built in 1878. Polebarn House is seen as it was before it was remodelled by the county council in 1920, with its cladding of ivy, its decorative balls and urns and the large cupola on the roof. It was built for the Revd John Clark, clothier and minister of the Tabernacle church, in 1789.

BOTH BUILDINGS ARE little changed. Polebarn House, now the Polebarn Hotel, lacks its cupola, but the urns and balls were recently restored with a grant from the Trowbridge Historic Buildings Committee. The Carpenters' Arms is one of the town's oldest remaining pubs, licensed in the early eighteenth century, when a carpenter called Thomas Herbert owned it. For many years there were workshops at the back of the pub. When Usher's Brewery acquired it in 1898, they altered the front part of the old building to what we see today.

CHURCH WALK

IT IS BELIEVED that a new church was built on the site of the present one in the twelfth century, on the far side of the market place from the castle gates. It is likely that the churchyard would have been surrounded by domestic and parish church secular buildings, as in other towns; for example,

an ancient building, the home of the church sexton, stood in a corner of the churchyard until 1859. However, it was not until the early nineteenth century that a paved way, separated from the adjoining churchyard, was made, providing a site for a variety of smaller shops and businesses.

THE IRON POSTS have gone though Church Walk remains, strictly for pedestrians only. The railings and gates of the churchyard went to satisfy the wartime demand for scrap iron, but the buildings are virtually unchanged. At the rear of the building nearest to us is a yard still paved with the pitched, or cobbled, paving that was once a fairly common feature of the town.

Nos 9 AND 10 CHURCH STREET

W.H. SIMS BEGAN his business in Roundstone Street, and later also at 12 Church Street. He was not at Nos 9 and 10 Church Street, as shown in the photograph, until about 1890. Earlier this building had been used by George Hanks, umbrella, parasol, patten, clog and trunk maker, who was there around 1850, and later by William Bath, umbrella and trunk maker. The umbrella trade was continued during the Sims' ownership; after the stone tile roof shown here was replaced by pantiles, the words, 'Ye Olde Umbrella Shoppe', were painted on the tiles in Gothic letters.

TROWBRIDGE STILL RETAINS several timber-framed buildings hidden by later frontages. In the eighteenth century particularly, it was fashionable to live in a Georgian house and if you did not have the money to build one then you added a modern frontage to your existing house, probably also hiding the fact that it had a pitched roof by extending the new façade upwards. The only house that still retains its original appearance is 9-10 Church Street, which has the typical combination of a hall range, built as a one-storey structure, along the street, and a cross wing of two storeys, the upper storey borne on a jetty. After deteriorating for many years, the building has recently been restored to a very high standard.

CHURCH STREET

THESE COTTAGES OF the late seventeenth or early eighteenth century projected out into Church Street, opposite the old rectory wall and between the parish churchyard and the Manvers Street Methodist Chapel. Their old brickwork, of local manufacture, had acquired a

warm orange glow, perhaps as a result of earlier colour washing. They were squeezed in between the street and the rear garden walls of Lloyds and the National Provincial banks, and were swept away for street widening in the 1950s.

BEYOND THE CAR park that is now on the site of the cottages we can see the building known as the Upper Vestry, built as an infants' school and vestry room for the parish church in 1861. The upper floor is still used for church purposes, and the lower floor is let as offices. In the distance of both photographs, on the left, is the former Parochial School, erected in 1846 and now converted to accommodation. The old rectory and the mulberry tree, under which the poet and rector George Crabbe used to write, were demolished in 1961; a new rectory and church hall have since been built on the site, and the road has been further widened.

CONIGRE CHURCH

CONIGRE UNITARIAN CHURCH was built in 1857, on the site of an earlier chapel of around 1700. The architect was William Smith of Trowbridge. In the old photograph, taken in around 1900, we can see some of the other buildings in the Conigre. Those on the left, which were apparently very old, were pulled down during the Urban District Council's slum clearance

programme in 1935, while the houses opposite survived until after the Second World War.

CONIGRE CHURCH BECAME derelict, was vacated in 1972 and subsequently demolished. However, the Unitarian congregation continued to meet in a smaller building elsewhere in the town. The Gothic building to the left of the church, hidden by trees in the old photograph, was built in 1865 as the Sunday school. It is now used by the Bethel United Church of Jesus Christ.

SHAILS LANE

THIS LANE, RUNNING up to the fields now occupied by the Seymour estate, took its name from a family who lived there in the seventeenth century. This is the only known photograph showing it as it was before the main Conigre demolition of 1935. On the right is The Harp Inn. Opposite the covered cart is the entrance to what is now called Riverway, known officially when this picture was taken as Gasworks Lane; to many older people it is known by the ancient, and rather picturesque, name of 'Gooseacre'.

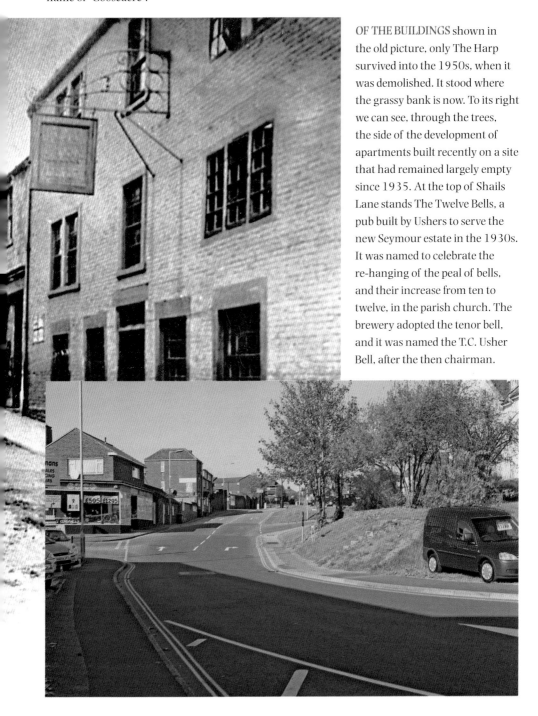

OF THE BUILDINGS shown in the old picture, only The Harp survived into the 1950s, when it was demolished. It stood where the grassy bank is now. To its right we can see, through the trees, the side of the development of apartments built recently on a site that had remained largely empty since 1935. At the top of Shails Lane stands The Twelve Bells, a pub built by Ushers to serve the new Seymour estate in the 1930s. It was named to celebrate the re-hanging of the peal of bells, and their increase from ten to twelve, in the parish church. The brewery adopted the tenor bell, and it was named the T.C. Usher Bell, after the then chairman.

THE CONIGRE – FROG LANE

THESE BUILDINGS WERE on the corner of Frog Lane and Church Street. It is difficult for any but those old enough to remember it to visualise the street pattern at this point in the town. Left of this picture ran two roads at different levels, separated by a row of buildings, some of which faced one way and some the other. The lower, usually called Frog Lane, led up to British Row; the upper, called simply Conigre, ran up past the two Broad Streets to a dead end near the Conigre Parsonage. All this was swept away in 1955 so that roads could be widened in preparation for a bus station.

FOR YEARS A blank wall replaced the group shown in our earlier picture. This has now been replaced by a Sainsbury's. Further up we see the side of the early nineteenth-century Fernleigh House. A feature that came and went at this point, between 1955 and the present, was a graceful bridge, high over the street. The bridge was used to carry a pipe for conveying beer between Back Street and British Row, both sites of Ushers' Brewery.

LOWER AND UPPER BROAD STREET, THE CONIGRE

TAKEN DURING THE demolition of 1935, the old photograph shows how the clearing of houses revealed the back of a group of buildings which had once been the Coach and Horses public house. Behind them is the still intact north side of Upper Broad Street. Most of this went too, but the large Georgian house continued to accommodate Diplock's Printing Works until it closed in 1956. The Conigre Pump, provided in 1842 for local householders and water carriers, still stood, although its top, now in the Trowbridge Museum, had been removed.

THE UPPER PART of the Conigre area still remains a car park in 2012, though it is likely to be built on soon. In the 1935 picture we glimpse the side of the Conigre Parsonage, built about 1700 and given to provide a home for the minister of the Conigre General Baptist church in 1729. After decades of dereliction, it has now been handsomely restored.

DUKE STREET

ALL THE HOUSES on the north side of Duke Street, including a small courtyard called Unity Square, were pulled down during the 1950s and '60s, making way for an extension of Lester's Garage, whose AA and RAC signs can be seen on the other side of the street. Some probably dated from the first development of Duke Street in the 1690s, and others are early nineteenth-century rebuilding. Note the Cotswold-style stone slates on the roof of the house and the charming

bow-windowed, small-paned shopfront. Facing the bottom of Duke Street, the Co-op central grocery store had already lost its gabled attic windows. However, it still had its proud inscription, 'TROWBRIDGE CO-OPERATIVE INDUSTRIAL AND PROVIDENT SOCIETY LIMITED', in projecting stone letters, cut when the store was built in 1865. This was laboriously scraped off by the then Co-op authorities in the 1960s, because they felt it wasn't in keeping with the modern image they wanted to portray.

AFTER MANY YEARS as an open space on which cars were displayed for sale, this brownfield site has been used to provide retail premises at the corner of Church Street and apartments, which can be seen in the foreground of the photograph. The former Co-op has recently been very handsomely restored, and the improvement of this part of the town continues with the building of groups of small houses to replace the former brewery premises in Duke Street.

YERBURY ALMSHOUSES, ROUNDSTONE STREET

THE PICTURESQUE YERBURY Almshouses were probably built in 1698 and were endowed by members of a family that had made money in the cloth industry during the previous 150 years. They provided accommodation and a small weekly sum of money for eight widows. Adjoining

them was a paddock on which Yerbury Street was laid out in 1793. Beyond, the terrace of three-storey shops called Marlborough Buildings is dated 1878. Opposite, the wall belonged to the extensive garden of Lovemead House. The shop on the right was one building in a small terrace that included the Dove Inn.

IN 1914 THE old almshouses were replaced by the ones in today's view. They are no longer used as almshouses. Some years ago it became necessary for two groups of almshouses in the town to be sold so that those in Union Street and Polebarn Road could be adequately maintained. Opposite, the inexorable need for car parking has led to the disappearance of the garden and houses, though much of the wall, which is probably contemporary with the eighteenth-century Lovemead House, remains. The milestone, with its iron plate stating '99 miles to London', which was in the wall has also been moved to another site.

SILVERTHORNE'S COURT

THIS COURT OF a dozen or more houses was one of a number of similar groups built in the seventeenth and eighteenth centuries in the back gardens of houses on the main street. It took its name from John Silverthorne, a baker who bought a house in Roundstone Street in 1714. The stone lower floors of the buildings were probably originally two-storey cottages, later given brick top storeys to provide workshop accommodation. In the 1950s they were used as a store.

THE COURT STILL exists as a shortcut between Roundstone Street and Duke Street; the last two inhabited houses in it went in 1962. Older people often called this court the 'drung', local dialect for a narrow passage.

THE CROWN AND
YORK BUILDINGS

THIS PICTURE IS one of several in an album labelled 'Trowbridge holiday 1904'. It shows
a carnival organized by men in the employ of Ernest Ireland, who had been engaged in the

construction of a sewerage scheme in the town for some months. Led by Kemp & Hewitt's Band, the parade started from the Crown in Timbrell Street, passing through many streets and eventually arriving in a field near the Ship, where sports, a comic cricket match and singing competitions were held. Amazingly, the idea had only been mooted earlier in the week, but all the men appeared in costume and each one was mentioned in the newspaper report. The upshot was a donation of £25 to the Cottage Hospital, believed to be larger than any single amount raised for it previously.

APART FROM THE interest of the occasion, the 1904 picture gives us a good view of York Buildings, a row of about twenty workers' cottages, dating from around 1820. They were demolished because they were on the projected route of a proposed inner relief road. In fact, this part of the road was never made, and the project has now been abandoned. The site of the houses remains vacant. The Crown, built in 1818, when this area was developed by Thomas Timbrell, remains open.

CORNER OF
TIMBRELL STREET AND
PROSPECT PLACE

IN THIS PICTURE we see, to the left, the end house of Timbrell Street, laid out in 1814 to provide a new entrance to the town from the north-east. It here joined what was until then the main road in this direction, joining the built-up areas of the Conigre and Islington but itself not built up at this time. The houses later built on it, seen to the right, were given the name of Prospect Place. In Timbrell Street, although the houses were built singly or in small groups by individual builders, a standard frontage with all sash windows was evidently required. In Prospect Place the houses have top-floor workshops with the typical long weaver's casements.

The pattern of the windows on the warehouse, with keystones at the shoulders as well as in the centre, can be seen on Studley Mill and Innox Mill in the town and enables us to date this building to 1860-70. It was built by a marine store dealer – nothing to do with ships but someone who bought and recycled metal, glass, rags, and bones.

TIMBRELL STREET AND Prospect Place, with the adjoining Thomas Street, Charlotte Street and Cross Street, formed a complex of workers' housing in 1815-20. In the 1960s its historical interest was quite unappreciated and almost all was demolished, being considered substandard. The site shown in this picture was left vacant to provide a route for part of the inner relief road, and only when the plan was abandoned did it become available for building. The new development shows a real effort to fit in with Trowbridge's older buildings.

WICKER HILL FROM
THE TOWN BRIDGE

TRADITIONALLY, WICKER HILL is believed to take its name from a fence that lined the end of
the ditch of Trowbridge Castle in the seventeenth and eighteenth centuries. It seems likely that

what was here, however, was an open watercourse running down Fore Street, in which the furthest buildings in the picture lie. The way in which the road curves to the Town Bridge and then back again shows how the ancient route ran down to a ford on the upper side of the bridge. Two of the most prominent buildings in this 1932 picture replaced earlier ones not long before. On the left is the former Town Bridge Garage, a motor showroom, which was built in 1915 by Barnes Brothers and remains much the same today. In the centre of the picture, the stone office block was built by the Pioneer Friendly Society in 1912.

IN THE MODERN photograph, the bridge, built in 1777 and subsequently widened, is still standing, now carrying the heavy traffic of today. Known as the Blind House, the stone lock-up on the right was built in 1758. In 1942 its roof was blown off by a bomb that fell nearby, but it was replaced after the war. The Pioneer Society Building was extended to the left in the 1930s. On the right, in the foreground, poor quality buildings from the post war period can be seen, but otherwise little has changed.

TOWN BRIDGE FROM STALLARD STREET

UNLIKE SO MANY of our pictures, this one shows no building that is still standing, unless we except the lower parapet wall of the Town Bridge, seen here from the bottom of Stallard Street. The group in the centre, once a dyehouse and, when this picture was taken, a warehouse and stables, was bought by the Local Board in 1889 and pulled down with the intention of rebuilding the bridge more in line with Stallard and Fore Streets. The little open space created was known to subsequent generations as Stanley's Park, after the town surveyor. To the right can be seen the end of

Bridge House, destroyed by a bomb in 1942 (luckily the main part of the building was restored); to the left can be seen the buildings replaced by the Town Bridge Garage and a building also destroyed by bombing on the same occasion.

THE BRIDGE STILL remains out of line with its approach roads, but we now have a footbridge just upstream from it, on the line that a new bridge might have taken. The former Town Bridge Garage bears the initials 'BB' for Barnes Brothers and the date 1915. It is a noteworthy survival: the showroom has changed very little since the early days of motoring.

SITE OF THE BEAR PUBLIC HOUSE, STALLARD STREET

IN THE EARLY eighteenth century houses on this site were held as a copyhold of the manor by successive John Rundles, father and son, who were gunsmiths. One of the houses was licensed by 1731, and the sign of the pub, the Blunderbuss, is known to have existed from 1757. The pub appears to have been rebuilt in the 1830s, and a new name, the Black Bear, later usually just the Bear, is recorded from 1839. In 1942 it was badly damaged by bombing. However, with large numbers of soldiers stationed in the town, pubs were doing good business and the Bear was patched up by removing the

damaged upper floor and putting on a flat roof. It continued in that form until 1955, when it was closed and demolished.

BEHIND THE BEAR lay the bacon and other meat products factory of Bowyers. Begun by Abraham Bowyer, a Trowbridge grocer, in around 1820, it occupied premises on this site from 1859 onwards. In 1953 it expanded by acquiring Innox Mill, the former cloth factory of Kemp and Hewitt. In today's picture, the large modern factory can be seen through the trees. To the right is the main building of the cloth factory, which was built in 1875, and a row of three stone houses built by a former clothier, James Cogswell, between 1856 and 1862.

TROWBRIDGE RAILWAY STATION

THIS 1905 VIEW shows the station staff. They would have included the men who ran the ticket and parcels offices on the station, and shunters, who handled the heavier traffic in the extensive marshalling yards nearby. Trowbridge still had an engine shed at this time; later a shunting engine came daily from the shed at Westbury. Porters would have helped passengers

with their luggage, and the station also had an out porter, who would deliver it in the town. Great Western Railway horse-drawn wagons, replaced later by lorries, were in action all over the area, delivering heavier goods.

INEXPLICABLY, THE 1848 station buildings and the adjoining goods shed of the same date were not listed. The buildings on the west (left-hand side in the modern photograph) platform were demolished in 1969, and those opposite, on a Sunday in 1984, on the unlikely grounds that they were unsafe. At that time British Rail promised that they would be replaced by a 'purpose-designed' building, but all that stands as yet on the near platform is a species of bus shelter. The goods yard was sold to Bowyers, who quickly demolished the goods shed on learning that an application to list it had been made.

THE STATION YARD

THE RAILWAY THROUGH the town, then called the Wilts, Somerset and Weymouth Railway, was built in 1848, and the station buildings shown here were of that date. The footbridge in the picture replaced a wooden one at the other end of the station in 1897. The vehicle like a stage coach was no doubt the omnibus provided by the George Hotel to meet the trains. The pigs would have been on their way to the bacon factory of Abraham Bowyer and Son, which adjoined the station yard to the right of the picture.

THE STATION IS still a busy one. Trowbridge has the advantage of being on two routes: trains from Cardiff, Bristol and Bath come through on their way to Weymouth via Yeovil, and to Portsmouth via Salisbury. The return service to Bath and Bristol is used by many commuters, so the extensive station yard provides much car parking space, while more has been laid out on the other side of the line.

BYTHESEA ROAD

THIS ROAD NAME gives rise to incredulous laughter from strangers to the town. It comes from a family who lived near Axbridge in Somerset, quite close to the Bristol Channel. In 1660 John Bythesea inherited Wyke House, a Jacobean mansion between Trowbridge and Staverton, which remained the family seat until 1832. Several members of the family prospered as clothiers in the town in the eighteenth century. Henry Bythesea, who lived in a fine house (formerly Bridge House) still standing in Stallard Street, acquired much of the land between the river and Newtown. In 1893 his descendent, Samuel Bythesea of Freshford, offered to give the town a new road across it, named after the family. He gave the horse trough to mark the coronation of Edward VII in 1902. It was never connected to a main water supply and relied on rainwater to fill it. By March 1937 it was deemed to be a traffic hazard and was demolished.

THIS PART OF Bythesea Road has been transformed by the erection in 2010 of the Shires Gateway, a row of prestigious shops on a site formerly occupied by a group of buildings once used as an iron foundry and later by the Wilts United Dairies; the company that became Unigate. On the right of the picture are the entrance to the Shires Shopping Centre, the Job Centre, and the Telephone Exchange.

MORTIMER STREET POST OFFICE AND BYTHESEA ROAD

ROBERT'S GROCER'S SHOP and the adjoining Mortimer Street post office were modern buildings when this picture was taken, *c.*1908. They were built to replace older houses in Mortimer Street when the entrance into the new Bythesea Road was made a few years earlier.

But the new road developed slowly. Two large villas, now used by the Ambra Project, still stand on the west side but a row of smaller houses on the east side has gone. In the picture we can see open land, still then used as allotments.

THE NEW ROAD continued to develop slowly in the 1920s and '30s. In 1923 a new football ground for Trowbridge Town was laid out where the allotments had been, a Drill Hall for the Territorial Army was built in 1926, and a grand new cinema, the Regal, was constructed in 1937. In 1934 the football club gave up their ground to provide a site for a new County Hall; the neo-Georgian County Hall was designed by P.D. Hepworth and opened in 1940. An extension to the south, built in 1977, is to become the town's new library. The laying out of the inner relief road in 1977 made it necessary to divert the southern end of Bythesea Road, so the grocer's shop and an adjoining bacon factory disappeared; trees forming a screen to the County Hall car park now stand on the site.

CRADLE BRIDGE

THE BRIDGE TAKES its name from a wooden footbridge across the river Biss; in 1850 it was replaced by a stone road bridge, which is still there, though widened on the north side. At this point the main river, used as a mill stream, was at a higher level than the overflow, crossed by a smaller bridge, which can be seen in the foreground of both photographs. This made the road on the Mortimer Street side lower than the main river and thus liable to flood after excessive rainfall. In spite of this, a row of houses was built in around 1820, which must have been flooded regularly until they were demolished in 1977. Three at the right-hand end were used as the Three Horseshoes pub, and some had parallel grooves in the doorway sides so that lengths of timber could be fitted to keep the water out.

IN THE BACKGROUND of the old photograph is a part of Victoria Mill, a factory built in 1835. It formed part of a large complex of factory buildings used to manufacture cloth until 1974. The owners built a modern extension to the factory on what had previously been a green paddock. It was used for a period by Peter Black Cosmetics and has now been derelict for some years. The trees on the left surround an extension to the County Hall complex, built in 1977. The wall on the right is part of the boundary of the early nineteenth-century Longfield House, which now, with the two bungalows in its grounds, is an island in the middle of a large and busy roundabout.

MORTIMER STREET

MORTIMER STREET WAS begun in 1815 on a piece of ground called Longfield running from Cradle Bridge to the top of Dursley Lane. It consisted almost entirely of workers' houses of two storeys; why those with another storey as a weaver's workshop, of which there were so

many at the other end of town, were almost absent at this end is not known. At the time of this photograph, around 1905, the tall building on the left was the London Inn. On the right is a disused pump at the entrance to New Road.

ONLY ONE ROW of original houses survives behind the camera. Otherwise the only old building we see is the Lamb Inn, licensed since around 1820. All the rest has gone; on the left for the expansion of County Hall, on the right for a mixture of housing and commercial premises (the latter now disused), and, further down the hill, to provide for today's traffic needs.

NEWTOWN AND
THE SHIP CORNER

AN AUSTRALIAN MILITARY band leads a parade along Newtown during the First World War. The troops behind the band have white bands round their caps, indicating that they are officer cadets from the training unit at Trowbridge Barracks. The poet Edward Thomas was stationed here

in 1916 after he had applied for a commission in the Royal Artillery. He was commissioned as a 2nd Lieutenant in November and, after final firing practice at Codford, he embarked from Southampton. He was killed by the blast of a shell during the first hour of the Arras offensive on 9 April 1917. Like many British poets, his voice was ended by the First World War.

THE HOUSES ON the left were built in the last decade of the nineteenth century after the sale of the Bythesea family's estate. On the right, in the distance, we see the houses called Mortimer Terrace, built in 1875, and the Ship Inn, which has been licensed since around 1840. The houses on the other side of Newtown are earlier and the row to the right, just out of the picture, is called Waterloo Terrace, providing a good indication of its date of building.

NEWTOWN

BUILDING BEGAN ON the west side of Newtown from 1790 onwards, part of the expansion of
the town which came with the introduction of machinery into some sections of the woollen

industry at that time. This is the only known view of the houses further away from the camera on the left, showing that they were of a similar three-storeyed type to the ones we see more clearly. The land opposite only became available for building on in the 1890s, so we have an interesting contrast between two groups separated in time by about a century.

MANY TERRACES OF three-storeyed houses, of which the top floor was a weaver's workshop, were demolished as 'sub-standard' in the 1950s and '60s, but the nearer part of the group in Newtown remains intact. The Rising Sun, of which we see the sign in the early picture, ceased to be a pub several years ago but it has retained its public house façade.

GLOUCESTER ROAD

IT IS AN interesting feature of Trowbridge's history that although the population stayed
virtually the same between 1830 and 1930, a number of new streets were built. These provided
homes for families who had previously been crowded in courts and yards, many built behind
older houses in the town centre. These new streets were mainly for working people – though
Westbourne Road (the entrance to which is behind the photographer in this 1930s view of

Gloucester Road) contained houses that were more for the 'lower middle classes'. The building facing the end of the road in both pictures is the Labour Club, built in 1924.

IN CONTRAST TO the earlier streets of workers' houses, the streets of this period, from the 1840s onwards, have survived almost complete. One feature that has largely disappeared, however, are the corner shops. The grocer's shop in the older picture was one of three in this road; on the corner of Westbourne Road was a general shop and post office, while on the corner with Newtown, at the bottom of the road, was a fairly large Co-operative store. At the junction with Bond Street was a butcher's shop, while in Bond Street itself there was a large bakery and shop, a sweet shop, and another grocer's. Nearby, in Newtown, the shops included an off-licence, a newsagent's and general store, a fish, poultry and game shop, another butcher's, and a dress shop. Local people had no need to walk into town for everyday shopping.

THE BARRACKS,
FROME ROAD

A BARRACKS WAS built in Trowbridge in 1794: no doubt because it was felt that troops might be needed to control the town's turbulent working population. It was intended for cavalry, and

45255 Trowbridge, R.A Barracks

the original building, seen here, provided stables below and living quarters above. After the Napoleonic Wars it was sold, but it was repurchased at the time of the Chartist disturbances in 1839, and remained in regular military use until after the Second World War. Between the wars a battery of the Royal Horse Artillery was stationed in it. In the 1950s its high walls, topped with broken glass, were a familiar sight for post-war children, but at least once a year they were allowed inside its gates. The main annual carnival procession started here, where it was judged before wending its way to the Park.

LIKE SO MANY other buildings, Trowbridge Barracks, a little changed example of military architecture from 1794, might have been thought to merit preservation had it survived for another twenty years. However, it was demolished in 1961, and the site at the corner of Frome and Bradley Roads was used for a mixture of houses and commercial premises. To the left of this photograph, one of the old boundary walls remains.

Other titles published by The History Press

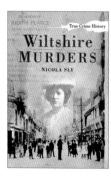

Wiltshire Murders
NICOLA SLY

Wiltshire Murders brings together numerous murderous tales, some which were little known outside the county, and others which made national headlines. Contained within the pages of this book are the stories behind some of the most heinous crimes ever committed in Wiltshire. They include the murder of Eliza Jones, stabbed to death by her common-law husband in 1836; the shooting of a policeman in 1892; and Mary Ann Nash, who disposed of her illegitimate son in 1907 by dropping him into a disused well.

978 0 7524 4896 1

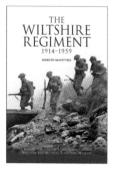

The Wiltshire Regiment 1914–1959
MARTIN MCINTYRE

Focusing on the period between the First World War and 1959, the date of the regiment's amalgamation with the Royal Berkshire Regiment when they formed the Duke of Edinburgh's Royal Regiment (Berkshire and Wiltshire), this painstakingly researched book uses over 200 photographs to vividly document the Wiltshire Regiment's role in many campaigns and battles from the trenches on the Western Front to terrorists in Cyprus in 1959, from Shanghai through to the Second World War.

978 0 7524 3757 6

Historic Gardens of Wiltshire
TIMOTHY MOWL

In a county of iconic landscape gardens such as Wilton, Stourhead and Longleat you'd think there would be few other gardens worth writing about. Yet this countrywide series proves that the more we search in the archives and in the hidden corners of each shire, the more rewarding are the surprises. Charles Bridgeman's geometric amphitheatres in the thickly wooded slopes at Amesbury and at Trafalgar House, Alderman Beckford's almost underwater grottoes at Fonthill and the grotto of the setting sun at Bowden Park all await discovery.

978 0 7524 2893 2

In Wiltshire's Skies
COLIN CRUDDAS

In 1911, Larkhill became Britain's first military airfield. Along with similar flying training bases constructed nearby, it was to occupy a cornerstone position in Wiltshire's early aviation history. It was these establishments, in addition to those at Gosport, Eastchurch, Farnborough and Montrose, that formed the only Royal Flying Corps and Royal Naval Air Service aerodromes in the British Isles when war was declared in August 1914. *In Wiltshire's Skies* throws a wide net over the locations, events and many colourful personalities which have shaped the county's aeronautical heritage.

978 0 7524 3235 9

Visit our website and discover thousands of other History Press books.

www.thehistorypress.co.uk